WITHDRAWN BY
WILLIAMSBURG REGIONAL LIBRARY

Major League SOCCER

New York City FC

Joanne Mattern

Mitchell Lane
PUBLISHERS

2001 SW 31st Avenue
Hallandale, FL 33009

www.mitchelllane.com

Mitchell Lane
PUBLISHERS

Copyright © 2019 by Mitchell Lane Publishers. All rights reserved. No part of this book may be reproduced without written permission from the publisher. Printed and bound in the United States of America.

Printing   1   2   3   4   5   6   7   8

Major League SOCCER

Designer: Ed Morgan
Editor: Sharon F. Doorasamy

Library of Congress Cataloging-in-Publication Data

Names: Mattern, Joanne, 1963- author. | New York City FC (Soccer team)
Title: New York City FC / by Joanne Mattern.
Description: Hallandale, FL : Mitchell Lane Publishers, 2019. | Series: Major League Soccer | Includes bibliographical references and index.
Identifiers: LCCN 2018003129| ISBN 9781680202502 (library bound) | ISBN 9781680202519 (ebook)
Classification: LCC GV943.6.N45 M38 2018 | DDC 796.334/64097471--dc23
LC record available at https://lccn.loc.gov/2018003129

PHOTO CREDITS: Design Elements, freepik.com, Cover Photo: Black/Corbis via Getty Images, p. 5-7 freepik.com, p. 8 SounderBruce/Flickr CC-BY-SA-2.0, p. 11 Arturo Pardavila III/Flickr CC-BY-SA-2.0, p. 12 Arturo Pardavila III/Flickr CC-BY-SA-2.0, p. 13 Simon Heseltine CC-BY-SA-2.0, p. 17. freepik.com, p. 18 Tim Clayton/Corbis via Getty Images, p. 21 Michael Stewart/Getty Images, p. 22 Fred Kfoury III/Icon Sportswire/Corbis via Getty Images, p. 23 Andes/César Muñoz CC-BY-SA-2.0, p. 25 freepik.com, p. 26 Brandon Wade/Getty Images

Contents

Chapter One
Major League Soccer 4

Chapter Two
How New York City FC Started 10

Chapter Three
Playing Our Game 16

Chapter Four
New York City FC's Best Players 20

Chapter Five
Communicating On and Off the Field 24

What You Should Know 28
Quick Stats 28
Timeline 29
Glossary 30
Further Reading 31
On the Internet 31
Index 32
About the Author 32

Words in **bold** throughout can be found in the Glossary.

Major League Soccer

CHAPTER ONE

What sport is played by more than 240 million people? The answer is soccer. This sport is the most popular sport in the world. Anywhere you have open space and a ball to kick, you can have a soccer **match**!

Soccer has been huge in other countries for generations. The sport first came to the United States during the 1850s. Immigrants from Europe brought the game to their new homes in United States.

Professional soccer was never as popular in the United States as baseball, football, or basketball. However, thousands of children played soccer in youth **leagues** all over the nation. Interest in the sport grew, and in 1968, the first U.S. professional soccer league formed.

The new league was called the North American Soccer League (NASL). The league included 17 clubs. NASL clubs had players from the United States and from Europe. However, some of the NASL's rules were different from soccer leagues in other countries. The league also had financial problems. Finally, in 1984, the NASL went out of business. But interest in soccer stayed strong.

Meanwhile, soccer fans in other nations were obsessed with the World Cup. The World Cup is the biggest soccer championship in the world. Every four years, soccer teams from all over the world compete to see which is the best. The World Cup is played every four years and is hosted by a different country each time.

Chapter One

The United States wanted to be part of the World Cup. Finally, in 1994, the governing body, Federation Internationale de Football Association (FIFA), agreed to let the United States host the World Cup. But there was a catch. As part of the deal, the United States promised to start a professional league. That league would follow the same rules as all other countries. The United States agreed and Major League Soccer (MLS) was formed in late 1993. It took a few years to put together teams and find places for them to play. The first Major League Soccer season was in 1996.

When it started, MLS had 10 clubs. They were the Colorado Rapids, the Columbus Crew, the Dallas Burn, D.C. United, the Kansas City Wiz, the Los Angeles Galaxy, the New England Revolution, New York/New Jersey MetroStars, the San Jose Clash, and the Tampa Bay Mutiny.

By 2017, MLS, had gotten much bigger. That year, MLS had 22 clubs. Nineteen of the clubs are from the United States. Three of the clubs are in Canada. The clubs are divided into Eastern and Western **conferences**.

Major League Soccer

Clubs in the Eastern Conference are the Atlanta United FC, the Chicago Fire, the Columbus Crew FC, the D.C. United, the Montreal Impact, the New England Revolution, the New York City FC, the New York Red Bulls, the Orlando City FC, the Philadelphia Union, and the Toronto FC.

The Western Conference clubs are the Colorado Rapids, FC Dallas, the Houston Dynamo, the LA Galaxy, the Minnesota Untied FC, the Portland Timbers, Real Salt Lake, the San Jose Earthquakes, the Seattle Sounders, Sporting Kansas City, and the Vancouver Whitecaps FC.

The clubs in MLS are from the United States and Canada. However, players from all over the world are members of MLS clubs. In 2017, MLS clubs included players from 67 countries. After the United States and Canada, most players come from Latin American and African countries. Players also come from Europe and Asia.

Each MLS club has 18 players on its game day **roster**. These players can take part in that day's game. A roster can have up to eight players from other countries.

Chapter One

Players report to training camp in January. They practice their skills. They learn to work together as a club. There might be new players on the club. Every year, clubs hold a **draft**. Many talented players are drafted to join the different clubs in the league. Players have to play for the team that drafts them.

The MLS season lasts from March to October. There are 34 matches in a season. Twenty-three of those matches are against clubs in the same conference. The other 11 games are played against clubs in the other conference.

In November, the top five clubs from each conference play in a 12-game **playoff** series called the MLS Cup Playoffs. Each conference starts with a **knockout round**. Then a series of **semifinals** and **finals** narrow the competition down to one club from each conference. Those top two clubs meet in the MLS Cup Championship in December. The winner of the MLS Cup receives the Philip F. Anschutz Trophy. This trophy is named after one of the founders of MLS.

The Seattle Sounders were treated to a ticker-tape parade after they won the Philip F. Anschutz Trophy in December 2016.

Major League Soccer

Clubs also earn points for each win and tie during the season. The club with the most points wins an award called the Supporters' Shield.

MLS clubs can also play in the Canadian Championships and the CONCACAF Champions League. The CONCACAF includes clubs from Mexico, Central America, and Caribbean nations. The winner of the CONCACAF Cup qualifies to play in the World Cup.

Each of the 22 clubs in Major League Soccer has its own history and exciting moments. The New York City FC is one of newest clubs to make history.

Fun Facts

1 In most of the world, soccer is called football. Only the United States, Canada, Australia, and a few other countries call it "soccer."

2 "FC" stands for "football club."

3 The top five birthplace countries for MLS clubs in 2017 were:

United States	288 players
Canada	28 players
Argentina	24 players
England	22 players
Ghana	16 players

How New York City FC Started

CHAPTER TWO

The New York City FC are part of the Eastern Conference. The club was not one of the original clubs created when MLS started in 1996. Instead, the FC is an **expansion club**.

Major League Soccer had wanted a club in New York City back in 2006. After meeting with several different investors, MLS finally announced that Manchester City, a major club in the United Kingdom, would own the new MLS club. On May 21, 2013, the New York City FC was officially announced as MLS's newest club. The FC was the twentieth club in MLS.

The day after the FC announcement, the team named Claudio Reyna as its director of operations. Reyna had played with Manchester City. He was responsible for hiring coaches and recruiting players. In December, Jason Kreis was announced as the first head coach. He had previously coached the MLS team Real Salt Lake.

The first players to be named to the FC were from Europe. The first was David Villa from Spain. He had played for several Spanish clubs and had also appeared in three World Cups.

David Villa was the first player signed to the FC, and he has been their best player ever since.

Chapter Two

Khiry Shelton shows his moves in a match against the Houston Dynamo in May 2015.

The second player named to the team was Frank Lampard. Lampard had played for teams in the United Kingdom. The FC's third player was Andrea Pirlo from Italy. In 2015, the FC chose a player from Colorado named Khiry Shelton in the MLS draft. He was the first American player to join the team.

New York City FC's first season started with an **exhibition** match against Scotland. David Villa scored FC's first goal and the FC won the match. The team's first MLS game was played on March 8, 2015. FC played Orlando City. The game ended in a 1–1 tie.

On March 15, FC won its first home game by defeating the New England Revolution. A huge crowd of more than 43,000 watched the match. The FC then slumped to an 11-game losing streak. Finally, on June 16, the FC defeated the Philadelphia Union. New York City FC ended the season with a disappointing 10-17 record and placed eighth in the Eastern Conference.

How New York City FC Started

The 2016 season saw Patrick Vieira step in as coach. He led the team to a 15-10 season. They were second in the Eastern Conference and fourth in the MLS. The FC went on to play in the MLS Cup Playoffs but lost in the semifinals.

The FC continued its winning streak in 2017. At the end of the 2017 season, their record was 16-9-9, and they finished in second place in the Eastern Conference.

The New York City FC's official colors are navy blue, sky blue, and orange. The blue colors are the same colors used by the Manchester City club. Orange was chosen to honor New York City's Dutch heritage and is also a color in New York City's flag.

FC's official home jersey paired a sky blue shirt with white shorts. The club's badge appeared on both the shirt and shorts. The team's jersey for away games was a black shirt with sky blue and orange trim. Five black stripes represented the five boroughs of New York City.

Patrick Vieira became the second FC coach in 2016.

Chapter Two

In 2016, the FC revealed a new away uniform. The shirt, shorts, and socks were navy blue trimmed in orange. The shirt featured sky blue circles that were meant to celebrate New York City's energy. The away uniform changed again in 2017. Now players would wear a sky blue shirt with navy blue shorts. The front of the shirt has a small New York City flag.

New York City FC's badge was originally a sky blue circle with the name of the club printed in navy blue and white letters. Before the team's first season began, fans were asked to choose the official badge. The winner was modeled on the old New York City subway tokens. The badge featured cut-out letters "NYC" in the middle and the name of the club in a circle.

How New York City FC Started

Since it began in 2015, New York City FC has played all its home games at Yankee Stadium in the Bronx, New York City. The team is working to build its own soccer stadium next to Yankee Stadium.

The New England Revolution has a loyal fan base. The FC's fans love to attend their games! Average attendance during the first three years was more than 26,220. When the team was in the MLS playoffs in 2016, an average of 28,000 fans saw the team play.

The FC has an official fan support group called the Third Rail. The name comes from the "third rail" that powers the New York City subway system. Club members hope to power the team in the same way. The Third Rail has its own section in Yankee Stadium and has more than 1,600 members. New York FC fans love their team.

Fun Facts

1. David Villa has been the FC's top scorer in all three seasons.

2. Although he played for a British team, Reyna was from New Jersey. He had also played for the MLS club the New York Red Bulls.

Playing our Game

CHAPTER THREE

Each soccer club has 11 players on the field. One player is the goalkeeper. His job is to guard the goal and block shots from the other club. The goalkeeper is the only player who is allowed to use his hands to block a shot or catch the ball.

The other 10 members of the club are usually divided into four defenders, four midfielders, and two forwards. However, clubs can change the 4-4-2 lineup at any time.

Defenders usually stand near the goal. Their job is to defend the goal. They block shots or move the ball away from the goal.

Midfielders play in the middle of the field. Midfielders can play both **defense** and **offense**. When their club is trying to score, they move forward with the ball. When their club is trying to stop the other club, they move back on defense.

Goalkeeper (GK)
Right back defender (RB)
Left back defender (LB)
Center back defender (CB)
Left midfielder (LM)
Center midfielder (CM)
Right midfielder (RM)
Left forward (LF)
Right forward (RF)

Forwards are offensive players. They move the ball forward to the other club's goal. The striker plays down the middle of the field. Wingers play on the sides. They try to feed the ball to the striker so he can score.

Mascots are another important part of a soccer club. Even though mascots don't play, they are often on the field to help fans get excited. Mascots also take part in giveaways and contests. They pose for pictures and sign autographs. They also take part in community events.

The New York City FC does not have an official mascot. However, one of the team's nicknames is the Pigeons because there are a lot of pigeons in New York City. The pigeon has become the unofficial mascot of the team. A pigeon mask is sometimes worn by fans.

Chapter Three

Like all sports clubs, New York City FC has a **rivalry** with some of the other clubs in the league. The club's main rival is the New York Red Bulls. The clubs have played against each other many times, and there is always a lot of energy on the field and off. Fans sometimes call the rivalry between the teams the Hudson River Derby.

Whether two clubs are rivals or just opponents, it can be a challenge to play a game on the other club's home field. Playing at home often means the stands are full of your club's fans. These fans support the club by cheering, waving signs, and other actions. However, when a club plays at an opponent's stadium, the fans are there to cheer for the other club. Often, fans will shout at the visiting club and try to distract players from the game. This is especially true in New York, where fans can be very loud.

A diehard New York City FC fan shows his support during a match.

Playing our Game

Another reason playing on another club's field can be difficult is the club is not familiar with it. Although soccer fields are standard, each stadium has its own features. Other factors, such as weather or altitude, can make things hard for a visiting club.

New York City FC may be a new club, but it is a strong one. The team has a winning record and many great players. Stars like David Villa are an important part of the team and so is new talent. The FC develops new players by working with local youth soccer clubs. The team also has a **youth academy** for players that are 13 or 14 years old. Those players may well be the FC stars of the future.

Fun Fact

The New York City FC has several nicknames. They include the Pigeons, the Bronx Blues, the Blues, and the Boys in Blue.

New York City FC's Best Players

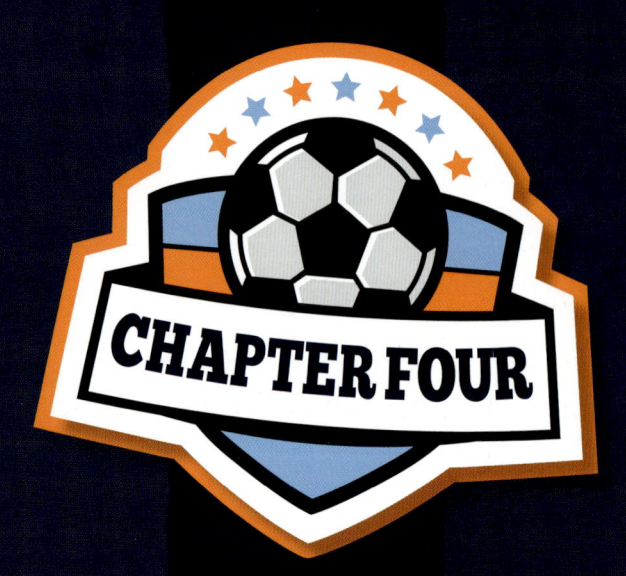

CHAPTER FOUR

The New York City FC is a new team, but it has some great players. Here are some of the FC stars:

David Villa
Forward (2015–present)
David Villa was the first player signed to the FC, and he is their best. Playing as a forward, he was the team's leading scorer from 2015–2017, and he also won **MVP** honors in 2015 and 2016. He has scored an average of 17 goals a season and plays in almost every game. In 2016, he was named the Most Valuable Player in MLS after scoring 23 goals that season.

Frank Lampard
Midfielder (2015–2016)

Midfielder Frank Lampard is another powerhouse player for the FC. In 2016 he scored 12 goals in 19 games. He also had three **assists** and 21 shots on goal. Before joining the FC, Lampard played on many top teams in the United Kingdom, including West Ham United, Chelsea, and Manchester City. He also played in three World Cups during his time with teams in the United Kingdom. He retired from soccer early in 2017.

Frank Lampard skillfully controls the ball during a match against the Columbus Crew in October 2016, his last season in MLS.

Chapter Four

Patrick Mullins
Striker (2015-2016)

With eight goals scored in 21 games played, Mullins was a key part of the FC during its first two seasons. He played as a striker. In July 2016, he was traded to D.C. United, but fans still remember his hard work during the FC's first season.

Patrick Mullins swerves around a New England player to gain control of the ball during a July 2015 match.

New York City FC's Best Players

Andrea Pirlo sets up a play during a 2017 match.

Andrea Pirlo
Midfielder (2015–present)

Pirlo came to the New York City FC from Italy during the FC's first season. He plays midfielder. Pirlo is best known for setting up plays that lead to goals and has been called one of the greatest playmakers. Pirlo is also great at scoring on **free kicks**. He was named to the MLS All-Star Team in 2016.

Communicating On and Off the Field

CHAPTER FIVE

Soccer is an international sport with players in almost every country on Earth. New York City FC, like all MLS clubs, has players from all over the world. Not all of these players speak English. You might think that players would have trouble communicating with each other. However, there are usually very few problems.

At the start of the 2017 season, the New York City FC had 28 players on its roster. Eleven of the players were born in the United States. One was from Canada. The other players were born in other countries, including Norway, Spain, France, Italy, Luxembourg, and England. Six players came from Central or South America. They were born in Costa Rica, Panama, Venezuela, Peru, Argentina, and Trinidad. And one player came from Finland. That's a lot of difference languages and cultures.

Communication is key in soccer, as in any sport. Players have come up with many different ways to talk to each other on and off the field. Sometimes they don't even need words. Soccer has been called a universal language. Players who understand the game do not need words to communicate with each other on the field. They just need know how to read signals and what plays they should do. They use body language and signs to understand what is going on.

Many soccer athletes have traveled quite a bit to play the game. An athlete might go to a soccer youth academy camp in a country different from his own. Often they travel to other countries to play for teams there. Along the way, these players pick up important words and phrases in their new language. Of course, they learn important soccer words and directions, too. It also helps that many foreign players learn English in school. This is especially true in Europe, Africa, and Asia.

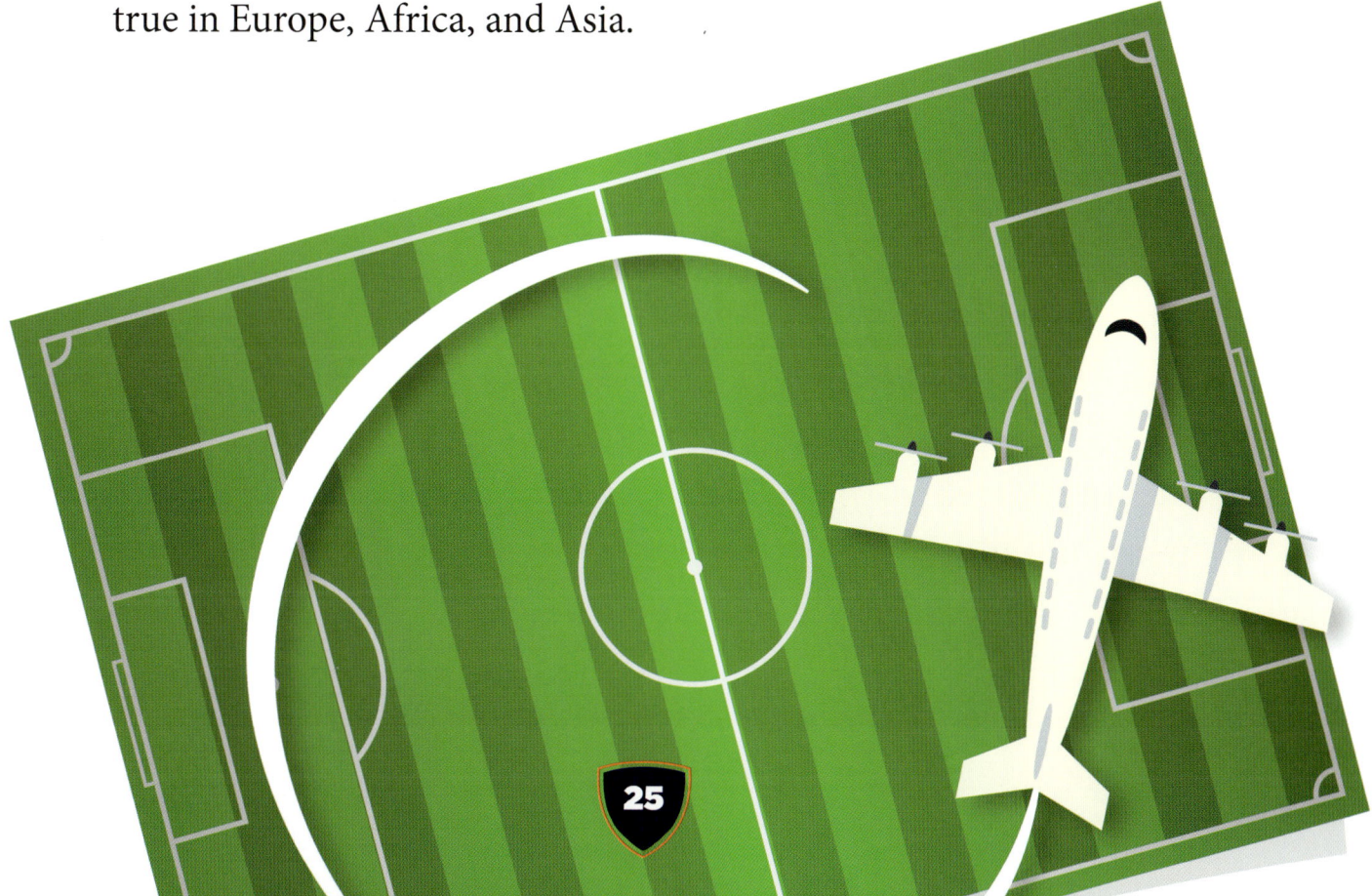

Chapter Five

Players aren't the only ones who need to communicate with each other. So do **referees**. Referees usually speak English, even during World Cup games. They also use different colored cards to warn players about **penalties**. Yellow cards warn the player that he has done something wrong and has to be careful. Red cards mean the player does not get another chance. He has to leave the field right away. Referees give red cards for serious violations, such as fighting, a violent foul, or other unsportsmanlike acts.

Players don't always agree with the referees. Milton Rodriguez of the FC Dallas confronts a referee after receiving a yellow card.

Communicating On and Off the Field

No matter what language a player speaks, it can be difficult to adjust to playing in a new country. The United States is different from other nations. The U.S. is a very large country, so foreign players have to get used to increased travel time. Instead of taking a bus from one game to the next, a team might fly for many hours to get to their next game.

The United States is large geographically, which means that MLS players must adjust to different weather and climate conditions. An MLS club may play in snow or ice one week. The next week may see them playing in a hot, humid climate. Foreign athletes have found that MLS soccer has many challenges but also many rewards.

Fun Fact

Altitude can also be a factor. The Colorado Rapids play in a stadium that is a mile above sea level. Real Salt Lake's stadium is also above 4,000 feet. That means the air is thinner there than at other clubs' home fields. The thin air can affect players' ability to breathe and make them feel tired or sick.

What You Should Know

- Mix Diskerud scored New York City FC's very first MLS goal.

- In 2015, five FC players represented their home countries in international competition.

- Chris Wingert has played the most minutes in his FC career.

- Josh Sanders played the most minutes in the FC's first season (2015).

- Of the top 10 MLS jersey sales in 2015, four were New York City FC players. Andrea Pirlo led the team in jersey sales that year.

- Khiry Shelton was the first substitute in FC history.

- The FC's first practice in 2015 was held in Florida, probably because it was too cold in New York City.

- David Villa is the only FC player to win MLS Player of the Week.

- Thomas McNamara is the only FC player to win MLS Goal of the Week.

- In 2015, the FC led MLS in penalty goals.

Quick Stats

David Villa played in 91 MLS games from 2015–2017, and scored 68 goals.

2015: Highest home attendance at an FC game: 48,047 on June 28.

2015: Highest away attendance against Orlando City FC: 62,510 on March 8.

2016: Between June 25 and July 6, the FC scored 3 straight shutouts.

2016: The FC make it to the MLS Conference Semifinals

New York City FC Timeline

2010
Major League Soccer officially announces there will be an expansion team in New York City.

2013
Manchester City agrees to be the owners of the new team; the New York City FC is officially announced.

2014
David Villa signs on as the FC's first player; Frank Lampard and Andrea Pirlo also join the team; the FC partner with local soccer teams to develop new players.

2015
The FC picks Khiry Shelton as its first American player in the 2015 draft; the team plays their first game; the FC creates its own youth academy.

2016
Patrick Vieira is named the new head coach; New York City FC makes it to the MLS Conference Semifinals.

2018
The FC hope to play in a new stadium next to Yankee Stadium.

Glossary

assists
Helping another player score a goal

conferences
Groups of sports clubs within a league

defense
Players who try to keep the other club from scoring in a game

draft
To choose young players to join a sports league

exhibition
A display of skill

expansion club
A club that is not one of the original clubs in a league but that is added later

finals
The playoff round that determines which clubs will face each other in the championship

free kicks
Chances to kick a ball into the goal as a result of a penalty against the other team

jersey
A shirt worn by a player on a sports team

knockout round
The playoff round that determines which clubs move on to the semifinals

leagues
Groups of sports clubs that play each other

mascots
A person or animal that symbolizes a club

match
A soccer game

MVP
Most valuable player

offense
Players who try to score in a game

penalties
Punishments given to players or a club for breaking rules

playoff
A game to determine which clubs will go on to the championship

professional
Doing something for money rather than as a hobby

referees
People who enforce the rules during a game

rivalry
Intense competition between two clubs

roster
A list of players on an MLS club

semifinals
The playoff round that determines which clubs move on to the finals

substitute
A person serving in place of another

youth academy
A training school for young players that is run by a professional soccer club

Further Reading

Kortemeier, Todd. *Total Soccer*. Minneapolis, MN: Abdo Publishing, 2017.

Laughlin, Kara L. *Soccer*. Mankato, MN: The Child's World, 2016.

Rausch, David. *Major League Soccer*. Minneapolis, MN: Bellwether Media, 2015.

On the Internet

Get Active with MLS
http://getactivewithmls.com/kids

MLS Soccer
http://www.mlssoccer.com

New York City FC
http://www.nycfc.com

Index

Canadian Championships 9
CONCACAF 9
CONCACAF Champions League 9
D.C. United 6, 7, 22
Diskerud, Mix 28
Eastern Conference 6-7, 10, 12, 13
FIFA 6
Hudson River Derby 18
Kreis, Jason 11
Lampard, Frank 12, 21
Major League Soccer (MLS)
   beginnings 6
   original clubs 6
   current clubs 6-7
   season 8
Manchester City 10, 11, 13, 21, 29
McNamara, Thomas 28
MLS Cup 8
Mullins, Patrick 22
New England Revolution 6, 7, 12, 15
New York City FC
   formation of 10-11
   first season 12
MLS Cup Playoffs 13
club colors 13
club badge 13-14
club uniforms 13-14
home stadium 15
attendance 15
fan clubs 15
mascot 17
nicknames 17, 19
rivalries 18
New York Red Bulls 7, 15, 18
North American Soccer League (NASL) 5
Pirlo, Andrea 12, 23, 28, 29
Reyna, Claudio 11, 15
Sanders, Josh 28
Shelton, Khiry 12, 28
soccer positions 16-17
Vieira, Patrick 13, 29
Villa, David 11, 12, 15, 19, 20, 28, 29
Western Conference 6-7
Wingert, Chris 28
World Cup 5-6, 9, 11, 21
Yankee Stadium 15

About the Author

Joanne Mattern is the author of many books for children on a variety of subjects, including sports, history, and biography. She has written many books for Mitchell Lane. Joanne loves to learn about people, places, and events and bring historical figures to life for today's readers. She lives in New York State with her husband, children, and several pets.